D0934423

Kevin Durant

SUPERSTARS IN THE WORLD OF BASKETBALL

SUPERSTARS IN THE WORLD OF BASKETBALL

Kevin Durant

Shaina Indovino

Mason Crest

Mason Crest
450 Parkway Drive, Suite D
Broomall, PA 19008
www.masoncrest.com

Printed and bound in the United States of America.

First printing
9 8 7 6 5 4 3 2 1

Series ISBN: 978-1-4222-3101-2
ISBN: 978-1-4222-3107-4
ebook ISBN: 978-1-4222-8797-2

The Library of Congress has cataloged the
hardcopy format(s) as follows:
          Library of Congress Cataloging-in-Publication Data

Indovino, Shaina Carmel.
   Kevin Durant / Shaina Indovino.
      pages cm. — (Superstars in the world of basketball)
   ISBN 978-1-4222-3107-4 (hardback) — ISBN 978-1-4222-3101-2 (series) — ISBN 978-1-4222-8797-2 (ebook) 1. Durant, Kevin, 1988—Juvenile literature. 2. Basketball players—United States—Biography—Juvenile literature. I. Title.
   GV884.D868I54 2015
   796.323092—dc23
   [B]
                              2014007849

Contents

KEY ICONS TO LOOK FOR:

Text-Dependent Questions: These questions send the reader back to the text for more careful attention to the evidence presented there.

Words to Understand: These words with their easy-to-understand definitions will increase the reader's understanding of the text, while building vocabulary skills.

Series Glossary of Key Terms: This back-of-the book glossary contains terminology used throughout this series. Words found here increase the reader's ability to read and comprehend higher-level books and articles in this field.

Research Projects: Readers are pointed toward areas of further inquiry connected to each chapter. Suggestions are provided for projects that encourage deeper research and analysis.

Sidebars: This boxed material within the main text allows readers to build knowledge, gain insights, explore possibilities, and broaden their perspectives by weaving together additional information to provide realistic and holistic perspectives.

Words to Understand

amateur: Playing a sport without getting paid.

passive: Accepting whatever happens without taking action.

aggressive: Ready to fight to succeed.

varsity: A sports team playing for a high school or college.

FAMILY SUPPORT

Tensions are high as the most talented players in the NBA run across the court. One of Kevin's teammates passes him the ball. He takes a deep breath before making a mad dash for the basket. He slides past his opponents and jumps up to score a slam dunk. The ball easily drops through the basket. It all happens so fast that his opponents aren't even sure what hit them. The fans clap and cheer, but not for long. The game is still under way.

Kevin Durant is playing in the 2012 All-Star Game, being held in Orlando, Florida. The game's players are chosen in a vote by their fans. The teams are divided into Eastern players and Western players. Kevin is on the West team, because he plays for the Oklahoma City Thunder, which is in the western division. His all-star teammates include Chris Paul, Kobe Bryant, Blake Griffin, and Andrew Bynum.

Kevin was named the Most Valuable Player (MVP) of the All-Star Game. It was easy to see why. He scored 36 points, 7 rebounds, and 3 assists in the game. Kevin was given a large glass trophy and asked how it felt to become an MVP at such a young age. He said, "It's a dream come true. I'm just blessed to be here."

Kevin has done amazing things in his time in the NBA. But he had to work hard to become the superstar athlete that fans know today.

KEVIN DURANT

Everything Kevin said was true. He dreamed of joining the NBA since he was a little boy. In his first year as an NBA athlete, he was named Rookie of the Year. He later became the NBA scoring champion three years in a row and even earned an Olympic gold medal. At the age of twenty-three, he wasn't ready to slow down. "I'm glad I'm taking this back to Oklahoma City," he added. Kevin has been a loyal member of the Oklahoma City Thunder since it was brought to the city in 2008.

CHILDHOOD

Kevin Wayne Durant was born on September 29, 1988, in Washington, D.C. He grew up in the nearby town of Seat Pleasant, Maryland. Kevin has two brothers, Tony and Rayvonne, and one sister, Brianna. When Kevin was still a baby, his father left the family and did not come back for over ten years. By then, Kevin was already a rising star in the sport of basketball.

Kevin's mother, Wanda, raised her children alone. Luckily, Wanda's mother, Barbara, was around to help. Wanda's children saw their grandmother a lot while they were growing up. Wanda needed to work overnight shifts at the post office to support her family. Someone needed to watch Kevin while she was gone. His grandmother offered to do it. When she wasn't around, Kevin's aunt Pearl took care of him and his brothers and sister. Sadly, Aunt Pearl died of breast cancer when Kevin was eleven years old.

Long before Kevin became the basketball superstar we know him as today, he stood out to his classmates for another reason. He was very tall, even as a kid. In fact, Kevin was always one of the tallest kids in his class. Wanda worried that her son would be treated differently because of his height. She was right. Kevin's classmates teased him for being so tall. Wanda tried to fix this problem by asking Kevin's teachers to place him at the end of school lines. She hoped fewer people would notice how tall he was. Wanda was always looking out for Kevin.

Kevin didn't like the attention he got for being tall and dreaded going to school. He thought his life would be a lot easier if he were the same height as everybody else. His grandmother believed something different. She told Kevin, "Someday, you'll like being

As a kid, Kevin played sports as much as he could with his brother Tony, dreaming of playing basketball in the NBA one day.

Make Connections

Charles "Chucky" Craig was easily one of the most important influences in Kevin's life. He was one of Kevin's first coaches. Chucky was killed when he was only thirty-five years old. Everyone who trained under Chucky was heartbroken when he died. Kevin always looked up to Chucky and wanted to honor him in some way. That is why he decided use the number 35—Chucky's age when he died—on his jersey. He used this number in the AAU, high school, college, and finally in the NBA. Kevin still uses the number 35 as a member of the Oklahoma City Thunder.

tall." Kevin knew his grandmother was right when he started playing basketball. Most basketball players are very tall. The extra height makes it easier to shoot a basket or block an opponent from shooting. By the time Kevin reached his full height of 6'9", he saw his height as a blessing and not a curse.

Wanda did her best to keep her children active. When Kevin was eight years old, his mother walked into the Seat Pleasant Recreational Center and signed Kevin and Tony up for weekend activities. Kevin and his brother played sports there on weekends. This is where Kevin met Charles "Chucky" Craig, his future coach. Chucky saw Kevin shooting hoops and knew that with a little training, Kevin could become a great basketball player. He invited Kevin to try out for the nine-and-under team he coached. Kevin scored 25 points in one of the first games he played.

DREAMS OF THE NBA

Kevin and Tony loved sports, but none more than basketball. They played basketball together and watched NBA games on television. One of their favorite teams was the Washington Wizards. Michael Jordan played for the Wizards.

Tony and Kevin played all sorts of sports throughout their childhood. Kevin eventually went on to play for a basketball team in the *Amateur* Athletic Union (AAU). The AAU includes many types of sports, not just basketball. The AAU even hosts Junior Olympic Games, which are held every year.

Any athlete knows the key to getting better is practice. Kevin began training when he was very young. His AAU coach trained him both on and off the court. One of his workouts took place on one of the steepest hills around Seat Pleasant. His coach made him run up the hill. When Kevin reached the top, he had to walk back down the hill, backward. When he reached the bottom, he had to run back up again. He did this over and over again, until his coach was satisfied.

Michael Beasley and Kevin became friends while they played for AAU teams, pushing each other to become the best players they could be.

Kevin remembers this exercise clearly to this day. He thinks it is a very important one. "When I have a son and he wants to play basketball, this is the first place I'm gonna send him," Kevin said in an interview. As a child, Kevin worked out for up to eight hours a day during the summer. He knows better than anyone that an athlete needs to work hard from an early age to become a great basketball player.

All of Kevin's hard work finally paid off when he was eleven years old and was playing for the Prince George Jaguars. The Jaguars made it to the finals of a national competition that year. During the second half of the final game, Kevin scored 18 points. That's a lot for an eleven-year-old! Thanks to Kevin and his teammates, the Jaguars won their first championship. That was the moment Kevin decided he wanted to join the NBA.

After Kevin told his coach of his plans to join the NBA, the Jaguars's coach, Taras Brown, asked, "Are you sure?" Taras asked because Kevin was very *passive* on the court. He didn't take many risks and didn't shoot the ball as often as he should. He had the skill to sink a lot of baskets at his age, but he simply wasn't doing it. Taras wanted to find out why.

Kevin told the coach he was sure. When asked why he didn't shoot as many baskets as he could, he said, "I didn't want to be the guy to take a lot of shots. I didn't want my teammates to be mad at me." Kevin didn't want to look like a ball hog. He understood that basketball is a team sport and didn't want to be selfish with the ball. Taras pushed Kevin to be more *aggressive* on the court, and it worked.

Kevin played for the Jaguars until 2003, when the team split up. During his time on the team, he met and played with two other great basketball players, Michael Beasley and Chris Braswell. All three players later joined the NBA. It is not uncommon for strong athletes to push their teammates to work harder and become better players. Michael and Kevin were great friends off the court. They ate breakfast together every day before getting on the bus to go to school.

Kevin's mother was always very involved in her son's life. She knew how serious Kevin was about joining the NBA and was determined to help him get there. Wanda worked

Kevin (left) listens to the national anthem with Team USA teammates LeBron James (center) and Kobe Bryant (right) at the Tomb of the Unknown Soldier in 2012. Today, like Kobe and LeBron, Kevin is one of the best basketball players in the world, but he had to work hard as a young man to be the player fans know today.

Text-Dependent Questions

1. What is an MVP? Why is impressive that Kevin won this award in 2012?
2. Why was Kevin made fun of in school? How did it help him later in life?
3. What did Kevin think was the most important exercise he did as a kid?
4. Why wasn't Kevin a very aggressive player when he was younger?
5. What other few NBA players did Kevin meet while he played for the Jaguars?

closely with Kevin's AAU coach to come up with the best training schedule for Kevin to follow.

Taras Brown grew very close to Kevin and his mother after many years. Kevin even began referring to Taras as his godfather. Taras never gave up on Kevin and even came up with a few rules for Kevin to follow. One of the most important was not to play any unofficial games. If he wasn't playing for a team, he wasn't allowed to play basketball at all.

After the Jaguars broke up, Kevin joined the DC Blue Devils. It was another AAU team. This team was filled with talented players, just like Kevin's last team. One of those players was Tywon "Ty" Lawson.

Before long, Kevin was ready to go to high school. It meant Kevin would take the next step on his way to an NBA career, playing on a *varsity* team.

Words to Understand

sophomore: The second year of high school or college.
retired: Put away and no longer used by new players.

BEFORE THE NBA

Kevin went to high school at the National Christian Academy. He set out to join the varsity team the moment he got there. Freshmen usually have a hard time making it onto the team, because they are smaller and less experienced than the other players. Coaches prefer stronger, bigger players. But Kevin was no ordinary freshman. He was very tall and extremely skilled for his age. His ability on the court was more than enough to earn him a spot on the team.

Kevin was noticed from the moment he started playing. It was obvious to everyone that Kevin would go far, but he did have one problem holding him back. His teammates didn't want to pass him the ball! Part of the problem was Kevin's attitude. When Kevin first started playing basketball as a high school student, he let his success get to his head. He started saying mean things to opponents on and off the court. This is known as trash-talking, and it is not a nice thing to do. Players should always be kind to their teammates and opponents, no matter how heated the game gets.

Ty Lawson played with Kevin when both players were in high school at the Oak Hill Academy. Both men would become huge stars in the NBA years later.

Another reason Kevin's teammates didn't want to pass him the ball was because of his age. Kevin was young, and the older players had more experience on the court. They didn't want Kevin to get all of the attention. Even if Kevin had a lot of skill, he didn't know what to expect in high school games. High school varsity teams played differently from AAU or middle-school teams.

Kevin touched the ball a lot more in his **sophomore** year. This brought him even more attention. He had finally become the shining star his family always knew he could be. The *Washington Post* named Kevin Player of the Year after his sophomore year.

FINAL YEARS OF HIGH SCHOOL

Kevin was off to a great start in high school. The National Christian Academy helped him gain popularity, and he was now known as one of the best high school players in his area. By his junior year, Kevin decided he needed a change. He transferred to Oak Hill Academy. Ty Lawson was also playing for the Oak Hill Academy. The two had met while playing for the DC Blue Devils in the AAU. Kevin and Ty were happy to play together once again.

As each year passed, Kevin took more steps toward his dream of joining the NBA. As a junior, his scoring average was much better than ever. He averaged over 19 points and 8 rebounds per game. This earned him a place on *Parade* magazine's All-American Second Team. By the end of Kevin's junior year, he felt he had learned everything he could at Oak Hill Academy. He was ready to move on yet again.

Kevin moved on to Montrose Christian School to complete his final year of high school. By now, he had reached his full height of 6'9". His average points per game increased to 23 in his senior year. And he averaged over 10 rebounds a game. Kevin spent his senior

Going to the University of Texas was a big change for Kevin, but soon he'd have the success on the court that would help him reach his goal of playing in the NBA.

year proving he was a skilled player in all areas of the court. He was named to the McDonald's All-American Team. In the 2006 McDonald's All-Star Game, he was named the co-MVP.

COLLEGE

Colleges all over the country had taken notice of the talented Kevin Durant. If Kevin went to college, he would be able to go on a sports scholarship. Sports scholarships are given to talented young athletes who choose to go to college. The only thing an athlete needs to do to keep the scholarship is get good grades and play for a sports team. In Kevin's case, he would be playing basketball, of course.

The choice to attend college was an important one for Kevin. Going to college had its advantages. College athletes gain more experience. If Kevin played for a college team, he would be able to travel all over the country and play against other colleges. NBA scouts would be more likely to notice him, as well. If he didn't go to college, he would have to wait a whole year before joining the NBA. Playing basketball in high school kept Kevin in shape. Waiting a whole year meant Kevin would have to work out on his own or join an amateur league.

Kevin thought a lot about his options. His former teammate Ty Lawson tried to get him to go to the University of North Carolina. Other colleges also wanted Kevin. In the end, Kevin picked the University of Texas. He set out to move there after completing his high school degree.

The move to Texas was not an easy one for Kevin and his family. Maryland and Texas are over a thousand miles apart. Going to college in Texas meant being far away from

Kevin became a star at the University of Texas, wearing his famous number thirty-five while showing basketball fans his skills.

his family. Wanda would miss her son, but she knew he needed to move to follow his dreams. Kevin had worked hard to get to this point, and nothing was going to get in his way.

Kevin was busy the summer before college. He worked out a lot to get ready for the upcoming season. By the start of his freshman year in college, Kevin was strong enough to be a starter. Besides being on court at the beginning of the game, starters also usually play during the most important parts of the game. As a starter, Kevin might be called in toward the end of the game to help score in the last few minutes.

The Longhorns did well with Kevin's help. They finished the season with 25 wins and 10 losses. Reaching the finals of the Big 12 Tournament was easy for the team, but the Longhorns did not win the title. They lost against Kansas and went home empty-handed. The Longhorns were invited to the NCAA Tournament. Kevin did well in these games, but it was not enough to win. It would take some time before the Longhorns were able to snag a championship title.

In team sports, there are offensive players and defensive players. Offensive players try to score points, while defensive players try to stop the other team from scoring. Kevin's ability to score a lot of baskets by being quick on his feet made him a great offensive player. Some freshman players take a long time to get used to the college league, but not Kevin. He averaged over 25 points and 11 rebounds a game.

By the end of his freshman year, Kevin had done everything he set out to do in college. He was named the Naismith and AP College Player of the Year. Kevin also received many other awards, including the John R. Wooden, Oscar Robertson, and Adolph F. Rupp awards. Being honored in this way is very rare for a freshman. Seniors, juniors, and even sophomores are more experienced and usually receive these awards. A freshman being named Player of the Year is almost unheard of!

Kevin's jersey number was retired after he left the University of Texas for the NBA so that no other player could wear his number, thirty-five.

Text-Dependent Questions

1. Why do freshmen in high school usually have a hard time getting on a varsity team?
2. What is trash-talking? Why was it a problem for Kevin?
3. What are the benefits of going to college for a professional athlete?
4. What is the difference between offensive and defensive players in basketball?
5. Why is it so rare for a college freshman to receive the Player of the Year award?

Kevin's college career didn't last very long. After a great first year, Kevin announced that he would be leaving Texas University to join the 2007 NBA draft. His former teammates, coaches, and family members all agreed Kevin was more than ready to play in the NBA. This is what he wanted all along, after all.

The University of Texas wished him luck in the NBA. The number 35 was *retired* as a way to honor the time Kevin spent at the university. Basketball players at the University of Texas will not be able to use that number again.

Words to Understand

prestigous: Of a very high status; inspiring respect.

OKLAHOMA CITY THUNDER

When a player signs up for the NBA draft, he is agreeing to join any team that picks him. It doesn't matter which team it is or how far away the team plays. The player has no choice in where he will play. The NBA lifestyle isn't for everyone. Players who enter the draft have trained their whole lives to get to this point and know what it means to become part of the NBA.

The NBA draft is held every June. Each team takes turns picking one athlete from the players who entered the draft that year. Teams with the worst record from the year before get to choose first. The teams with the best records choose last. This keeps every team as fair as possible.

Kevin Durant knew he would be one of the top picks in 2007. He hoped he would be the first pick, because that meant he would get to play with the Portland Trailblazers. That team was filled with great players, including Brandon Roy and LaMarcus Aldridge. Kevin had spent months wondering what it would be like to play with them.

Kevin signs a ball for a fan while practicing with the Seattle SuperSonics.

Some of the best athletes in the world endorse big sports companies. An endorsement is an agreement between a company and an athlete. Kevin signed an endorsement deal with Nike after he joined the NBA. He was paid to wear Nike's clothes and shoes. Sometimes, he even appeared in commercials. Athletes are paid a lot of money in endorsement deals. In Kevin's case, he was paid $60 million for a seven-year deal. That was on top of his annual salary with the SuperSonics! This was one of the largest endorsement deals made with Nike that year.

But Kevin wasn't picked first. Kevin was disappointed when the Seattle SuperSonics made him their first choice, but the second choice overall. Though it wasn't the Trailblazers, it wasn't long before Kevin began to like playing for the SuperSonics.

ROOKIE SEASON

Kevin wasted no time showing Seattle what he was made of. He packed his bags and moved to the West Coast to start his rookie year. Rookies are new to the NBA. It usually takes rookies a season or two to adjust to playing in a professional league. Kevin was different. He had been preparing for the NBA his whole life.

Kevin first played guard for the SuperSonics. Later, he played forward. There are two types of forwards: small forwards and power forwards. Small forwards are quick and aggressive. They can move toward the basket very fast. Power forwards have great shooting skills and have no problem making shots from anywhere on the court. Players who fill these roles are strong in every area of basketball. This includes scoring points, making assists and rebounds, and stealing the ball from the opponent. Kevin was able to play both forward positions with ease.

The 2007–2008 season started off well for Kevin. He scored 18 points and had 5 rebounds and 3 steals in his very first game. At the end of the season, he went out with a bang, scoring his first double-double. A double-double happens when a player scores double digits in two categories. In Kevin's case, he scored 40 points and 13 rebounds in one game. His scoring average for the season was over 20 points. Statistics like these earned him the Rookie of the Month award a few times that year. He finished the season as NBA Rookie of the Year. He also earned a spot on the All-Rookie First Team.

After playing with the Seattle SuperSonics, Kevin moved teams to play for the Oklahoma City Thunder in 2008.

OKLAHOMA CITY THUNDER

The Seattle SuperSonics made a very big decision in 2008. They chose to move from Seattle to Oklahoma City. Once the SuperSonics arrived in Oklahoma City, the team was renamed the Oklahoma City Thunder. Oklahoma is in the middle of the country. Kevin and his teammates were happy with the move.

The Oklahoma City Thunder was a brand-new team, even though it had a lot of experienced players. Kevin and his teammates had a new arena to play in, too. It was upgraded following the Oklahoma City bombing more than ten years earlier.

Oklahoma City was happy to have such a talented team. Kevin and his teammates would work their hardest to make Oklahoma City proud. That year, several new players were added to the team, including Russell Westbrook. He became one of the strongest players on the team, alongside Kevin.

The Thunder did not get off to a great start. There were several possible reasons. The entire team needed to move partway across the country. They were also playing in a new stadium with a new crowd. It would take time for the team to get used to playing in a new place. But by the end of the season, the Thunder was beginning to show its true colors. Kevin finished the 2008–2009 season with an average of 25 points a game. He scored about half the baskets he shot.

The Thunder's second year was much better than its first. Kevin and his teammates won a lot of games, including a nine-game winning streak. With more than 50 wins, the team even made it to the playoffs! The 2009–2010 season was very good for the Thunder, but the team still had a few areas to improve on if the Thunder ever wanted to make it to the NBA finals.

Kevin continued to get better, while the Thunder struggled to keep up. He really started

The Oklahoma City Thunder play at the Chesapeake Arena. Kevin has called the arena home since he started playing for the Thunder in 2008.

Make Connections

Kevin Durant became a member of the 50-40-90 club after the 2012–2013 season. He is one of six NBA players to ever join this club. The others are Steve Nash, Larry Bird, Mark Price, Reggie Miller, and Dirk Nowitzki. There are three requirements to get in. First, a player has to score at least 50 percent of all shots taken. This is where the 50 comes from. He must also score at least 40 percent of 3-point shots taken and at least 90 percent of free throws attempted. These averages must be made in the same season.

to make his mark on the basketball world in 2010. Kevin scored an average of 30 points per game and became the NBA scoring champion for the first time. An NBA player must score more points than any other player to become an NBA scoring champion. Kevin kept his title through 2012, becoming the scoring champion a total of three times in his career—so far.

Each year, the best players from the NBA are chosen to play against each other in a special basketball game known as the NBA All-Star Game. Fans choose the players for each team. They are divided into two teams based on where the player's team is located. There is a Western Conference and an Eastern Conference. Players from Oklahoma City, for example, play in the Western Conference and would be on the West team in the All-Star Game. Kevin was first selected to play in the NBA All-Star Game in 2010. He has been picked to play in this *prestigious* game every year since. Kevin was named the game's All-Star Most Valuable Player (MVP) in 2012.

Research Project

A rookie is a player who is new to the NBA. Usually, players don't do as well when they are rookies as they do when they are more experienced. Look up more information about Kevin's averages. How did his performance as a rookie compare to how well he did when he had been in the NBA for a few years? Look at some other players' records, too. Did they improve after they got past their rookie years?

Kevin's choice to stay with the Thunder in 2010 was a big one for the NBA superstar, but it paid off in the end.

Text-Dependent Questions

1. What is the NBA draft? Does a player have a choice about what team he joins?
2. Who gets to choose first in the NBA draft?
3. What is a double-double? Why is it impressive that Kevin was able to get one?
4. What does it mean that Kevin became the NBA scoring champion?
5. What is the All-NBA First Team? Who chooses it? Does the First Team actually play a game?

In 2010 Kevin was named to the All-NBA First Team for the first time. Basketball sportswriters and broadcasters choose the members of this team. The players chosen for the team do not actually play. Being selected means they are the best at their positions. As of 2013, Kevin had been named to the team a total of four times. If he continues to play well, Kevin will probably be selected to many more first teams!

Kevin had a very big decision to make in 2010. His contract with the Thunder was almost up. If he wanted to, he could leave the Thunder and become a free agent. Free agents can sign with any team that offers them a good deal. Before the 2010–2011 season began, Kevin made his decision. He re-signed with the Thunder for a much better deal than the one he had before. The contract would last for five years, and he would earn about $80 million for those five years. That's about $16 million a year!

The choice to stay with the Thunder was a good one. The team improved a lot during the 2010–2011 season and even made it to the Western Conference finals before losing to the Dallas Mavericks. The Oklahoma City Thunder did even better the next season. Kevin and his teammates led the Thunder all the way to the 2012 NBA finals. They faced the Miami Heat in the final games. They fought hard but lost in a series of five games. Kevin scored over 20 points in each game, averaging 30 points per game during the finals.

The Oklahoma City Thunder had a great start in the 2012–2013 season. Kevin was determined to make it to the finals again. Winning an NBA championship was one of the few things he had not done in his career. If the Thunder played as well as the year before, there was a shot at winning.

The team won 60 games that year, easily making it to the Western Conference playoffs. Russell Westbrook, one of the team's best players, was injured during the first game. Losing him made it very hard for the rest of the team to do well. Kevin did his best to lead the team alone, but it just wasn't meant to be. The Thunder didn't even make it to the NBA finals that year.

Words to Understand

compassionate: Caring strongly about others.

KEVIN DURANT TODAY

Kevin's first official international competition was in 2010. He joined Team USA to take on the International Basketball Federation (FIBA) world championship. It was held in Turkey that year. The U.S. team played some great games against the best basketball teams in the world. Kevin performed very well. During one game, he scored 38 points. He is the only member of Team USA to ever score that many points in a single FIBA game. Kevin also scored 7 3-point shots in the final game against Turkey, setting a world record.

Through a lot of teamwork, Team USA was able to win the 2010 world championships. This was a very important win for the United States, because it was the first time the team had won in sixteen years! Kevin and his teammates came home with a gold medal. Kevin's skills and talent did not go unnoticed. He was named the MVP of the tournament and added to the All-Tournament team.

Two years later, Kevin was given another opportunity to show the world what he was made of. He was invited to join Team USA in the 2012 Olympics in London. The Olympic

Kevin (right) jokes with Team USA teammates Carmelo Anthony (left) and Kobe Bryant (center) during the 2012 Olympics in Beijing.

Games are one of the biggest and most important competitions in the world. Being selected to play on the U.S. Olympic team is a very big deal.

The U.S. Olympic basketball team is made up of the best players in the NBA. The only way a player can become a part of Team USA is by being asked to join. Some of Kevin's teammates during the 2012 Olympics were LeBron James, Russell Westbrook,

Kevin and the rest of Team USA hear from Chairman of the Joint Chiefs of Staff U.S. Army General Martin E. Dempsey before the team plays a game for American soldiers in Washington, D.C.

Kevin takes a shot during a practice game with Team USA before the 2012 Olympics.

Kobe Bryant, and Carmelo Anthony. Kevin and his teammates made their country proud. The United States went undefeated and won the gold medal. Spain won the silver medal, and Russia took home the bronze.

PERSONAL LIFE

Family has always been very important to Kevin. His mother, Wanda; grandmother, Barbara; and aunt Pearl helped him get where he is today. They were very supportive through Kevin's toughest times. His aunt Pearl was a very important part of his life. Kevin was broken up after she died. When he finally joined the NBA, he started writing her name on his sneakers as a way to remember everything she had done for him.

Kevin lives in Oklahoma City and owns a large house in the area. He has thought about getting married soon. Kevin met Monica Wright while they were both in high school. They met during the 2006 McDonald's All-American Games. Like Kevin, Monica is a basketball player. She entered the WNBA draft in 2010 and was chosen second overall to play for the Minnesota Lynx. This team is very talented. The Lynx won the WNBA finals in 2011, while Monica was a part of the team. In July 2013, Kevin proposed to Monica. Kevin and Monica ran into some trouble in their relationship early in 2014. Only time will tell if they will be able to work out their problems.

When Kevin isn't practicing on the court, he has fun in other ways. Two of Kevin's favorite pastimes are movies and music. He is known to invite his teammates over to his house to watch movies like *Home Alone* and *Twister*. With some of the money he earned as a basketball player, Kevin bought expensive audio equipment. He even has his own personal sound studio.

Kevin is a Christian and takes it very seriously. Wanda often took Kevin to church when

The awful devastation left by the tornado that hit Moore, Oklahoma, inspired Kevin to give his time and money to help the people affected by the disaster.

he was growing up and taught him how important it was to pray to God. Kevin carries a Bible around in his backpack to this day. When something good happens, he thanks God. If something bad happens, he prays to God for help. Going to church helped Kevin get over some of the toughest times in his life.

Kevin is very active on the Internet. He has his own website, which includes a short biography, stories about his life and time in the NBA, and even a personal blog. It can be found at www.kevindurant35.com. The thirty-five in the address is from his team number, which he has used since he started in the NBA. Kevin also has Twitter and Facebook accounts.

MONEY AND DONATIONS

Basketball players make a lot of money. Kevin earns millions each year from his basketball salary alone. He also makes a lot of money from signing endorsement deals with different companies. Some of the companies Kevin has worked with are Nike, Sprint, Gatorade, and General Electric. He has even designed his own shoe.

In 2009 Kevin decided to give back to the recreational center that started it all. This was where Kevin had first met Charles "Chucky" Craig, his coach and mentor. He donated $25,000 to the center to help build a gaming room. It was filled with big televisions, couches, and Xbox 360 video game consoles. Kevin wanted the room made so that anyone who needed a place to stay would be comfortable. It would also give the children visiting the recreational center a place to hang out and relax.

A deadly tornado tore through Moore, Oklahoma, in 2013. It destroyed many houses and killed over a dozen people. Hundreds of people were injured. Kevin knew he needed to do something to help the community recover. He donated a million dollars to the American Red Cross to help the victims. Nike was so moved by Kevin's donation that the company decided to donate a million dollars as well. Nike-brand clothes and sneakers were given to the victims who needed the help.

Research Project

Kevin has given millions of dollars to help other people. Go online to find out what other NBA players have done to help those in need. List some of the charities that players have given to and explain what each organization does. Does the NBA as an organization do charity work as well? If so, what does it do?

Text-Dependent Questions

1. Why was it so impressive that the United States won the 2010 world FIBA championship?
2. Why did Kevin start writing "Pearl" on his sneakers when he joined the NBA
3. What is Kevin's religion?
4. Where does Kevin make money from, other than his salary as a basketball player?
5. How did Nike respond when Kevin donated $1 million to the American Red Cross?

The people of Moore, Oklahoma, were very thankful for Kevin's donation, but Kevin didn't feel he was doing enough. He wanted to help in a more personal way. He visited Moore and looked at the wreckage for himself. Kevin spoke with the people who were hurt by the tragedy. He signed shirts and basketballs for the victims in an effort to brighten their day. According to Monica Wright, Kevin Durant is a, "really **compassionate** guy." Whenever some sort of tragedy happens, he is always, "the first one who wants to help."

On the court, Kevin continues to push himself. He likes to play for a long time during each game so that he can help his team win. Kevin has learned to inspire his teammates through how well he plays and by what he says in the locker room.

Kevin has said he would like to work with kids after he retires from the world of professional basketball. But Kevin has no plans to slow down any time soon, at least not until he snags an NBA championship title!

Series Glossary of Key Terms

All-Star Game: A game where the best players in the league form two teams and play each other.

Assist: A pass that leads to scoring points. The player who passes the ball before the other scores a basket gets the assist.

Center: A player, normally the tallest on the team, who tries to score close to the basket and defend against the other team's offense using his size.

Championship: A set of games between the two top teams in the NBA to see who is the best.

Court: The wooden or concrete surface where basketball is played. In the NBA, courts are 94 feet by 50 feet.

Defensive: Working to keep the other team from scoring points.

Draft (noun): The way NBA teams pick players from college or high school teams.

Foul: A move against another player that is against the rules, mostly involving a player touching another in a way that is not fair play.

Jump shot: A shot made from far from the basket (rather than under the basket) while the player is in the air.

Offensive: Working to score points against the other team.

Playoffs: Games at the end of the NBA season between the top teams in the league, ending in the finals, in which the two top teams play each other.

Point guard: The player leading the team's offense, scoring points and setting up other players to score.

Power forward: A player who can both get in close to the basket and shoot from further away. On defense, power forwards defend against both close and far shots.

Rebound: Getting the ball back after a missed shot.

Rookie: A player in his first year in the NBA.

Scouts: People who search for new basketball players in high school or college who might one day play in the NBA.

Shooting guard: A player whose job is to take shots from far away from the basket. The shooting guard is usually the team's best long-range shooter.

Small forwards: Players whose main job is to score points close to the basket, working with the other players on the team's offense.

Steal: Take the ball from a player on the other team.

Tournament: A series of games between different teams in which the winning teams move on to play other winning teams and losing teams drop out of the competition.

Find Out More

ONLINE

Kevin Durant Humble in the Heartland
sports.espn.go.com/espn/otl/columns/story?id=6530509

Kevin Durant
kevindurant35.com

Kevin Durant: Biography
www.jockbio.com/Bios/Durant/Durant_bio.html

NBA Hoop Troop
www.nbahooptroop.com

Kevin Durant
twitter.com/KDTrey5

IN BOOKS

Doeden, Matt. *Kevin Durant: Basketball Superstar.* Mankato, Minn.: Capstone, 2012.

Fawaz, John. *NBA All-Stars.* New York: Scholastic, 2013.

Frisch, Aaron. *Oklahoma City Thunder.* Mankato, Minn.: Creative Education, 2012.

Herzog, Brad. *Hoopmania: The Book of Basketball History and Trivia.* New York: Rosen, 2003.

Schaller, Bob, and Dave Harnish. *The Everything Kids' Basketball Book: The All-Time Greats, Legendary Teams, Today's Superstars—and Tips on Playing like a Pro.* Avon, Mass.: Adams Media, 2009.

Index

About the Author

Shaina Indovino is a writer and illustrator living in Nesconset, New York. She graduated from Binghamton University, where she received degrees in sociology and English.

Picture Credits